JUL 30 2019

W9-BZO-459

21st Century Skills INNOVATION LIBRARY

UNOFFICIAL GUIDES

FORTNITE:
Beginner's Guide

CHERRY LAKE PUBLISHING • ANN ARBOR, MICHIGAN

by Josh Gregory

Published in the United States of America by Cherry Lake Publishing
Ann Arbor, Michigan
www.cherrylakepublishing.com

Reading Adviser: Marla Conn MS, Ed., Literacy specialist, Read-Ability, Inc.
Photo Credits: Page 4, ©JJFarq/Shutterstock; page 10, ©Wachiwit/
Shutterstock

Library of Congress Cataloging-in-Publication Data
Names: Gregory, Josh, author.
Title: Fortnite. Beginner's guide / by Josh Gregory.
Other titles: Beginner's guide
Description: Ann Arbor, Michigan : Cherry Lake Publishing, 2019. | Series:
    Unofficial guides | Series: 21st century skills innovation library |
    Includes bibliographical references and index. | Audience: Grade 4 to 6.
Identifiers: LCCN 2019003341| ISBN 9781534148185 [lib. bdg.] |
    ISBN 9781534151048 [pbk.] | ISBN 9781534149618 [pdf] |
    ISBN 9781534152472 [ebook]
Subjects: LCSH: Fortnite (Video game)—Juvenile literature.
Classification: LCC GV1469.35.F67 G742 2019 | DDC 794.8—dc23
LC record available at https://lccn.loc.gov/2019003341

Cherry Lake Publishing would like to acknowledge the work of the Partnership for
21st Century Learning. Please visit www.p21.org for more information.

Printed in the United States of America
Corporate Graphics

Contents

Chapter 1

Taking the World by Storm

Have you played *Fortnite* yet? Sometimes it seems like every person on earth is talking about this incredible game. Kids and adults love to play it and watch their favorite **streamers** in action.

In a short time, *Fortnite* has gone from just another video game to a global craze.

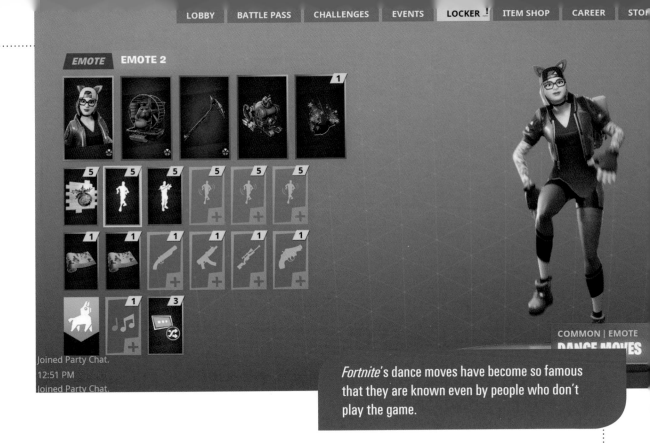

EMOTE   EMOTE 2

Joined Party Chat.
12:51 PM
Joined Party Chat.

COMMON | EMOTE

DANCE MOVES

Fortnite's dance moves have become so famous that they are known even by people who don't play the game.

Famous athletes, musicians, and actors discuss the game in interviews. Sometimes they even stream themselves playing with fans! And of course, anywhere you go, you might see people suddenly break out into famous *Fortnite* dance moves.

    Fortnite is truly a worldwide sensation. In a short time, it has gone from an experimental project by the **developers** at Epic Games to one of the most popular video games ever. Epic started working on the game in 2011. The company's developers wanted to combine the fast-paced, competitive fun of online shooting games with the creativity of building games such as *Minecraft*. After years of work, they finally released an early version of the game in July 2017.

Fortnite is set in a world where massive storms are sweeping across the land. At the same time, dangerous zombies are rising up and attacking people. In the original version of *Fortnite*, players team up to build bases and defend against zombie attacks. This mode, called Save the World, is still a part of the game.

Save the World and Battle Royale were the first two modes added to *Fortnite*.

Building is an essential skill in *Fortnite*, no matter which mode you are playing.

However, it was not until the addition of a mode called Battle Royale that *Fortnite* really took off.

Battle Royale was added to the game in September 2017. In this mode, up to 100 players at a time compete against each other to be the last one standing, instead of banding together to fight zombies. Players can build forts, towers, and other structures. At the same time, they can attack each other using a variety of weapons. Battle Royale became wildly popular almost immediately. Within two weeks of Battle

Royale's release, more than 10 million people had downloaded *Fortnite* so they could try it out. In less than a year, that number rose to more than 125 million. Even more incredibly, it is still growing.

Once most people try *Fortnite* for the first time, they are likely to keep on playing. According to Epic Games, about 80 million people play the game each month. This means it ranks among the top online games in the world in popularity.

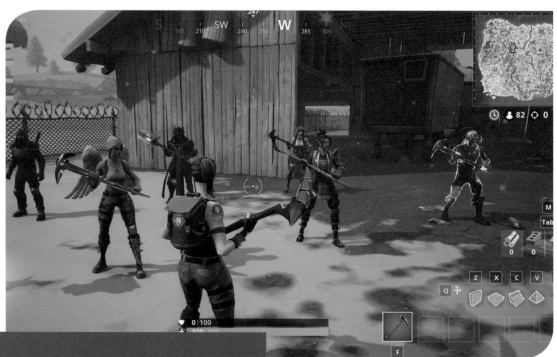

You'll never have any trouble finding people online to join you in a *Fortnite* match.

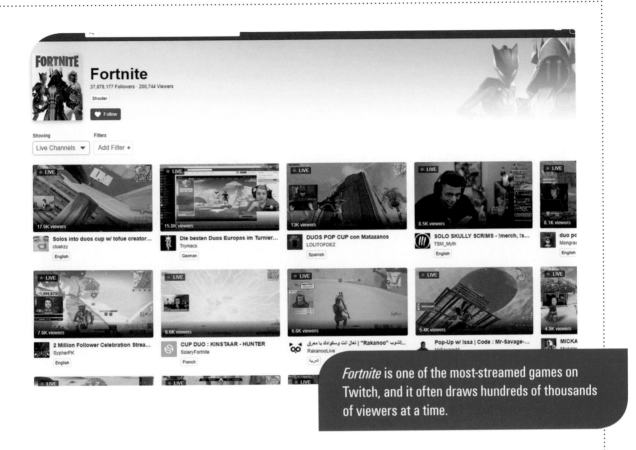

Fortnite is one of the most-streamed games on Twitch, and it often draws hundreds of thousands of viewers at a time.

Many people also enjoy the fun of *Fortnite* without actually playing the game themselves. The game is extremely popular on streaming services such as Twitch. Here, millions of fans tune in to watch live as the game's best players pull off amazing moves. *Fortnite*'s most famous players have even become worldwide celebrities!

Another big reason *Fortnite* has become so popular is that it is completely free to play. All you need to get started is a device that can play the game and an internet connection. *Fortnite* can be played on a Windows or Mac PC. It is also available for the PlayStation 4, Xbox One, and Nintendo Switch video game consoles. If you don't have any of those, you can play the game on an iOS or Android smartphone or tablet.

Simply download the game on the device of your choice and create an Epic Games account. The free version of *Fortnite* will let you play Battle Royale mode as much as you want. But even though the main game

With devices such as the Nintendo Switch, players can even enjoy *Fortnite* when they are on the go.

Even though *Fortnite* is free, you should always ask a parent or other trusted adult before you start playing. You will need to provide some basic personal information when you create an Epic Games account. You should always seek an adult's permission before you give away this kind of information online.

Your parents should also know when you are playing an online game with strangers. That way, they can help you if you run into any dangerous or uncomfortable situations while playing.

You'll also need to get permission if you want to spend money on skins, dances, Battle Passes, or other **microtransactions** in the game. After all, your parents won't be happy if they find a bunch of surprise *Fortnite* charges on their credit cards!

is free, there are still some parts of *Fortnite* that cost money. If you want to play Save the World, you will need to buy the full version of the game. Also, if you've played the game before, you know all about the cool outfits and dance moves you can unlock for your character. These extra features sometimes cost money too. But remember, none of them will have any effect on your ability to play the game and do well. They are just for looks. Don't worry if you can't afford them!

Chapter 2

Jumping In

Now that you know the story behind *Fortnite*, it's time to dive in and find out what all the fuss is about. Once you have the game installed, getting started is easy. Loading up Battle Royale mode will take you to a screen called the lobby. Here, you will see your character. Your character's appearance is random. It changes each time you play. If you are

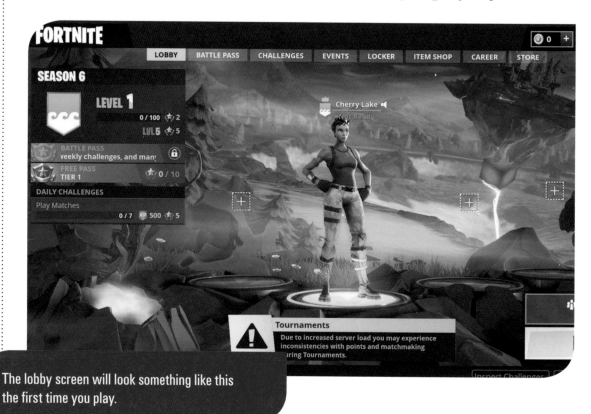

The lobby screen will look something like this the first time you play.

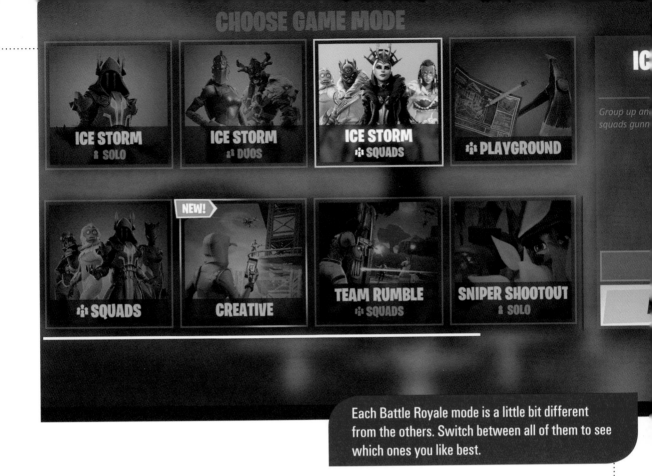

CHOOSE GAME MODE

ICE STORM
SOLO

ICE STORM
DUOS

ICE STORM
SQUADS

PLAYGROUND

ICE

Group up an
squads gunn

NEW!

SQUADS

CREATIVE

TEAM RUMBLE
SQUADS

SNIPER SHOOTOUT
SOLO

Each Battle Royale mode is a little bit different from the others. Switch between all of them to see which ones you like best.

playing in a group with friends, you will see their characters standing behind yours.

There is some information on the lobby screen that will become important after you have played for a while. But for now, let's just jump into your first match! First, you'll need to choose what kind of match you want to play. In Solo, you will be on your own against 99 other players. The last person standing wins the match. In Duos, you will team up with a partner. If you get knocked down, your partner will have a short time to heal you, so you won't get knocked out right away. Squads works the same way, except you will be on a team of four players.

In addition to these three main modes, there are also limited-time-only modes. These are added to the game from time to time. They can only be played for a limited time. Every so often, they are replaced with other unique modes. For example, in Food Fight, there are two teams of 12 players. One protects a pizza mascot, and the other defends a hamburger mascot.

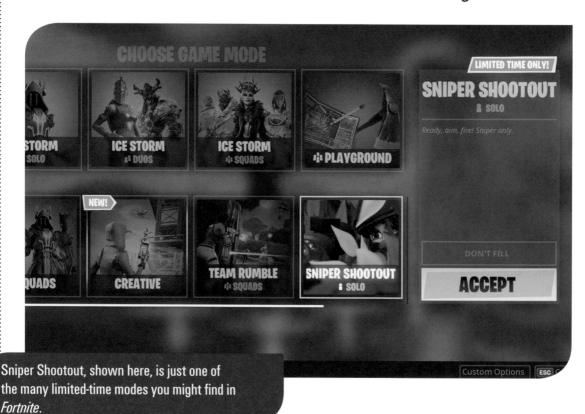

Sniper Shootout, shown here, is just one of the many limited-time modes you might find in *Fortnite*.

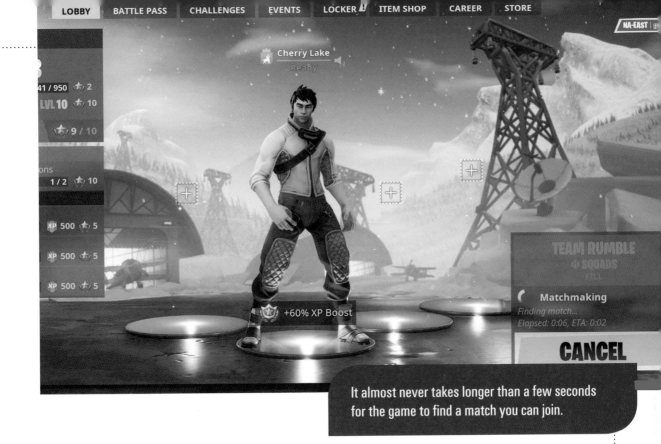

It almost never takes longer than a few seconds for the game to find a match you can join.

The first team to destroy the other's mascot wins. These fun modes offer some variety if you need a break from the main Battle Royale mode.

Unless you are playing with a group of friends, it is probably best to start with Solo. This will let you take your time and learn how to play. You won't have to worry about disappointing any teammates if you get knocked out early in the match!

Hit "Play" to start your first match. The game will start searching for a match you can join. This can take a few seconds, so be patient. Once the game loads,

Controlling the Action

The way you control *Fortnite* varies depending on which device you are using to play the game. On smartphones and tablets, you use touchscreen controls to do everything. On Windows and Mac PCs, you use a keyboard and a mouse or touch pad. On a video game console, you use a controller. Some players prefer one control style over the others. If you can, try playing *Fortnite* on different devices. Choose the one that feels most comfortable to you.

you will find yourself on a small island surrounded by other players. Some of them might be wearing cool costumes or carrying impressive weapons. Your first thought might be to fight them or run away. But don't worry! The match hasn't actually started yet. This is just a holding area where everyone waits for the game to fill up with 100 players. You can't take damage yet, even if someone starts firing weapons at your character. Take this time to get used to controlling the game. Run around and look in different directions. Swing your pickaxe. Search for guns to try out. You won't be able to bring them into the actual match. But you can practice while you wait.

Once the game has 100 players, you will suddenly find yourself flying through the air in a vehicle called the Battle Bus. Look around as the bus flies. You will see the world of *Fortnite* far below you. It is a large island with all kinds of interesting-looking areas. You might spot mountains, forests, towns, and other cool locations. Every match starts with the Battle Bus flying in a straight line across the island. As the bus flies, players will parachute out. This means every player gets to choose where they will start out on the map.

Picking a good starting point is an important part of succeeding in *Fortnite*, so think carefully before you

The Battle Bus's strange appearance is just one example of *Fortnite*'s wacky sense of humor.

jump out of the Battle Bus. Many players will jump out right away. They all end up clustered together. This means many of them will get knocked out near the start of the match. When you are just learning to play, it is a good idea to wait awhile before jumping. This way, you can find a less-crowded spot to start out.

Once you jump, you can skydive to fall faster. You can also open a glider. This will let you choose which direction to move as you fall. Your first thought as you are falling might be to head toward one of the towns

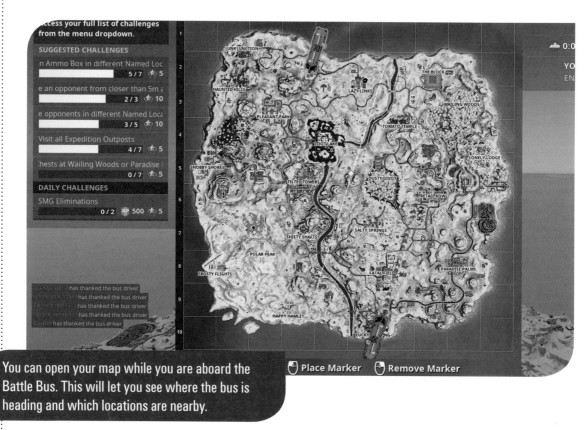

You can open your map while you are aboard the Battle Bus. This will let you see where the bus is heading and which locations are nearby.

Staying Safe Online

Most of the other people you play *Fortnite* with are likely to be strangers. If you are playing Solo mode, this is probably no big deal. Those players won't be able to talk to you or bother you outside the game. But if you choose to play in Duos or Squads, your teammates might talk to you. If these teammates aren't friends you know in real life, remember the rules of online safety:

- Don't reveal any personal information about yourself. This includes your real name, your hometown, the name of your school, or anything else a stranger could use to find you in real life.
- If a stranger says something that makes you feel uncomfortable, stop playing and tell an adult.
- Be nice to other players. Don't insult them or make fun of their skills. You don't want to ruin someone else's fun with a bad attitude.

or other interesting areas on the island. But keep in mind that many other players will have the same thought. These areas will be more crowded than forests, hills, or other outdoor areas.

If all goes well, you should land safely. Now it is time to start **scavenging**. You will start without any items except a pickaxe. Look around for guns, ammo, and healing items lying on the ground. Sometimes you will find loot boxes, which look like treasure chests.

You will also need building materials. There are three kinds: wood, brick, and metal. Sometimes you will find them lying on the ground. But the fastest way to get them is to use your pickaxe. You can knock down anything you see in the game. Hit a tree with your pickaxe. Hit a car. Hit a house. All of these things can be destroyed and turned into building materials!

After you are in the match for a little while, you will see an alert that the storm eye is shrinking. In *Fortnite*, there is always a dangerous storm

The game will always let you know how much time remains before the storm eye shrinks again.

surrounding the game world. As a match goes on, the storm eye shrinks. This means the game area will get smaller and smaller. Check your map when the storm eye starts shrinking. You need to get inside the white circle. If you don't, you will get caught in the storm. This will damage your character and eventually knock you out of the match, so be careful.

Now you know the basics of a Battle Royale match:

- Jump out of the Battle Bus and choose a starting location.
- Scavenge for items and weapons.
- Watch out for other players.
- Stay inside the shrinking storm eye.

This might sound simple, but keeping track of everything can take some practice. Once you have a good handle on how a match works, you can start paying closer attention to the details of the game.

Chapter 3

The World of
Fortnite

As you play your first few matches of *Fortnite*, you might feel overwhelmed with options. There are a lot of weapons and items to find. But you can't carry everything you find! Which things should you keep? Which ones should you leave behind? What is

Start each match by seeking out chests and other containers to find loot.

Cherry Lake

broncos51066

greensupp

xSwayyx

xSwayyx

greensupp

broncos51066

E Pick Up

PUMP SHOTGUN
★★

100

It is usually a good idea to pick up the first weapon you find, just in case you need it right away. You can always swap it for something else later.

the difference between all these items? Don't worry if you are confused at first. There is a lot to discover about *Fortnite*. You will learn everything you need to know as you keep playing.

The first thing you might want to do is get familiar with the game's different weapons. There are shotguns, pistols, sniper rifles, and many others. You can win matches using any type of weapon, so pick the ones you like best. But remember that you can't always predict which types of weapons you will find in a match. You should eventually try to get good at using all of them. This will allow you to do well in a match even if you can't scavenge your favorite weapons.

In addition to weapons, you should pick up a variety of healing items. Bandages and medkits heal your health points. Shield potions heal your shield points. Best of all are Slurp Juice and Chug Jugs. These items refill your health and shields at the same time. Don't try to use a healing item unless you are in a safe location. It takes a few seconds to use the item. You won't be able to fight during this time. This means you will be **vulnerable** to attacks.

A Chug Jug fully refills your health and shields. This is incredibly useful!

Most of the time, you will travel around the *Fortnite* island on foot. You can jog at a regular pace or sprint quickly. But there are other ways to get around the map. As you explore, you might get lucky enough to find a vehicle. Shopping carts are the simplest vehicles. They work best if you are playing in Duos or Squads. One player can push the cart while another rides inside, shooting at enemies.

The All Terrain Kart is a golf cart that can fit up to four players inside. One player drives, while others can shoot from the passenger seat. You can also jump on the roof to bounce high into the air.

Finally, there is the Quadcrusher. This four-wheeled vehicle can boost up to high speeds and crash through buildings. It can even smash enemies. It can carry a driver and one passenger.

As you start getting better with *Fortnite*'s weapons, you should also get used to building. Use your pickaxe to gather materials as you roam the island. You can build five main types of structures: walls, roofs, stairs, floors, and ceilings. Go to an area where there aren't any other players to bother you. Now practice fitting the different pieces together. Try building a tower to help you get up high. Keep at it until you can build quickly while moving and shooting at the same time. This skill will definitely come in handy!

Chapter 4

Getting Better

By now, you should feel right at home when you start a *Fortnite* match. You know what to do and where to go. You know how to find items and build structures. But you still can't win a match. The other players seem impossibly good!

Believe it or not, you can be just as good as those players. All you need to do is practice and pay careful attention to which strategies work best in different

At the end of each match, you can look at a report that shows exactly how well you played.

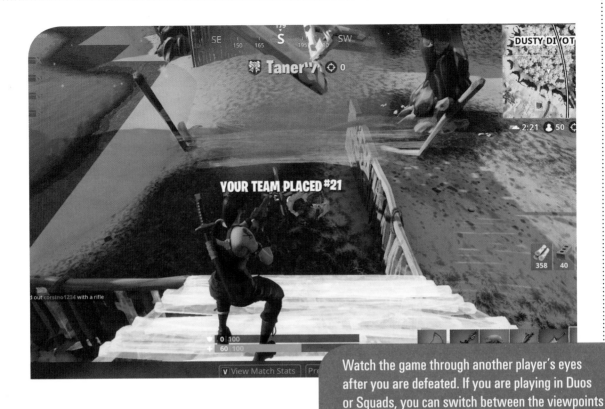

Watch the game through another player's eyes after you are defeated. If you are playing in Duos or Squads, you can switch between the viewpoints of different players on the team that beat you.

situations. Even when you are losing matches, you are learning from your mistakes. Think carefully about the match each time you get knocked out. What was the cause? Did the other player have better aim? This means you need to practice your shooting skills. Did your rival build a tower faster than you could keep up? Then you need to practice your building skills!

One great way to learn new things from a match is to watch what other players are doing. When you are defeated, the game will switch to show the screen of the player who knocked you out. Don't quit and go back to the lobby screen. Stay and watch what the other player does. You might be able to pick up a few new tricks! How do the best players move around the map? What kinds of things do they build? Which weapons do they use in different situations?

As you play more, you will find your fingers moving faster across your controller, keyboard, or screen. The controls will become second nature. You won't need to think about what you're doing. It will be as natural as walking or breathing!

With a little practice, you'll be well on your way to winning your first Victory Royale!

A Sneaky Way to Play

Do you find yourself getting knocked out early almost every time you start a new *Fortnite* match? One strategy you can try is to simply avoid fights. Remember that succeeding at *Fortnite* is not about defeating other players. Instead, it is about surviving longer than everyone else. Stick to the outer edges of the storm eye. Avoid running out into open areas. If you see other players fighting, back off. Let them knock each other out. With a little luck, you will find yourself among the final few players in the match!

Of course, this is where a match gets tricky. It is much harder to stay in the game when only the best players are left standing. And if you want to end up in first place, you will eventually need to fight at least one other player. But using this strategy is a great way to make it to the final part of a *Fortnite* match.

You will also soon know your way around the *Fortnite* island, as if it were your own neighborhood. You will barely need to look at the map once you learn where different landmarks are. You will start to understand which areas draw crowds of other players and where you will be able to stay hidden.

Remember, there is no wrong way to play *Fortnite*. Feel free to experiment and have fun. Play the game any way that feels right to you. Be creative and try your best. You just might discover a whole new way to play!

Glossary

developers (dih-VEL-uh-purz) people who make video games or other computer programs

microtransactions (mye-kroh-trans-AK-shuhnz) small pieces of video game content that are sold individually for low prices

scavenging (SKAV-en-jing) searching for useful items

streamers (STREE-murz) people who broadcast themselves playing video games and talking online

vulnerable (VUL-nur-uh-buhl) able to be attacked

Find Out More

BOOKS

Cunningham, Kevin. *Video Game Designer*. Ann Arbor, MI: Cherry Lake Publishing, 2016.

Powell, Marie. *Asking Questions About Video Games*. Ann Arbor, MI: Cherry Lake Publishing, 2016.

WEBSITES

Epic Games—Fortnite
www.epicgames.com/fortnite/en-US/home
Check out the official *Fortnite* website.

Fortnite Wiki
https://fortnite.gamepedia.com/Fortnite_Wiki
This fan-made website offers up-to-date information on the latest additions to *Fortnite*.

Index

About the Author

Josh Gregory is the author of more than 125 books for kids. He has written about everything from animals to technology to history. A graduate of the University of Missouri–Columbia, he currently lives in Chicago, Illinois.